THE UNTAMED WORLD

Tigers

E. Melanie Watt

RAINTREE
STECK-VAUGHN
PUBLISHERS

A Harcourt Company

Austin   New York
www.raintreesteckvaughn.com

Copyright © 2002 Weigl Educational Publishers Limited

All rights reserved. No part of the material protected by this copyright may be reproduced or utilized in any form or by any means, electronic or mechanical, including photocopying, recording, or by any information storage and retrieval system, without permission in writing from the copyright owner. Requests for permission to make copies of any part of the work should be mailed to: Copyright Permissions, Steck-Vaughn Company, P.O. Box 26015, Austin, TX 78755.

Published by Raintree Steck-Vaughn Publishers, an imprint of Steck-Vaughn Company.

Library of Congress Cataloging-in-Publication Data

Watt, E. Melanie.
   Tigers / E. Melanie Watt.
     p. cm. -- (Untamed world)
   Includes bibliographical references (p.).
   Summary: Describes the physical characteristics, classification, behavior, habitat, and endangered status of tigers.
   ISBN 0-7398-4973-5
   1. Tigers--Juvenile literature. [1. Tigers. 2. Endangered species.] I. Title. II. Series.

QL737.C23 M553 2002
599.756--dc21

2001048366

Printed and bound in Canada
1234567890 05 04 03 02 01

Project Coordinator
Heather Kissock
Substantive Editor
Leslie Strudwick
Raintree Steck-Vaughn Editor
Simone T. Ribke
Illustration and Layout
Warren Clark
Bryan Pezzi
Copy Editor
Diana Marshall
Photo Research
Joe Nelson

Consultants
Kathy Traylor-Holzer, Conservation Biologist, Minnesota Zoo, Apple Valley, Minnesota
Kathy Hornocker, Veterinary Coordinator, Hornocker Wildlife Institute, Bozeman, Montana

Acknowledgments
The publisher wishes to thank Warren Rylands for inspiring this series.

Photograph Credits
Corbis: page 40; **Corel:** cover, pages 4, 5, 6, 7, 15, 19, 20, 21, 30, 36, 41, 43, 59, 61; **Eyewire:** pages 32, 39; **Hornocker Wildlife Institute:** pages 8 (M. Hornocker), 12 (H. Quigley), 13 (H. Quigley), 14 (J. Goodrich), 18 (D. Miquelle), 22 (H. Quigley), 23 (K. Quigley), 24 (M. Hornocker), 25 (H. Quigley), 28 (M. Hornocker), 29 (M. Hornocker), 31 (H. Quigley), 44 (H. Quigley), 45 (H. Quigley), 55 (H. Quigley), 56 (H. Quigley), 60 (H. Quigley); **Photofest:** page 49; **Save the Tiger Fund:** page 57; **J. D. Taylor:** pages 11, 16, 33, 38, 42; **Visuals Unlimited:** page 34 (A. Copley); **E. Melanie Watt:** pages 17, 26.

Contents

Introduction 5

Features 7

Social Activities 17

Tiger Cubs 23

Habitat 29

Food 33

Competition 39

Folklore 49

Status 55

Twenty Fascinating Facts 59

Glossary 62

Suggested Reading 63

Index 64

Introduction

Today, there are fewer than 8,000 tigers in the wild.

Opposite: Current estimates indicate that there are between 5,000 and 7,500 tigers in the wild today.

The tiger, with its famous stripes, is the largest type of cat in the world. One hundred years ago, there were about 100,000 tigers in the wild. Now tigers are **endangered**. This means they are in danger of becoming extinct. Today, there are fewer than 8,000 tigers in the wild. In fact, three of the eight subspecies of tigers have become extinct in the last 30 years.

There are several kinds of tigers. In this book you will discover the differences between each of the tiger subspecies. You will read about the Siberian, or Amur, tiger. It is the biggest tiger of them all. You will also discover why some tigers treat humans as prey, and find out what is pushing this great cat toward extinction.

This book will help you understand the tiger and the world it lives in. You will learn what is being done to save the tiger and what you can do to help.

Tigers in the wild are found only on the continent of Asia.

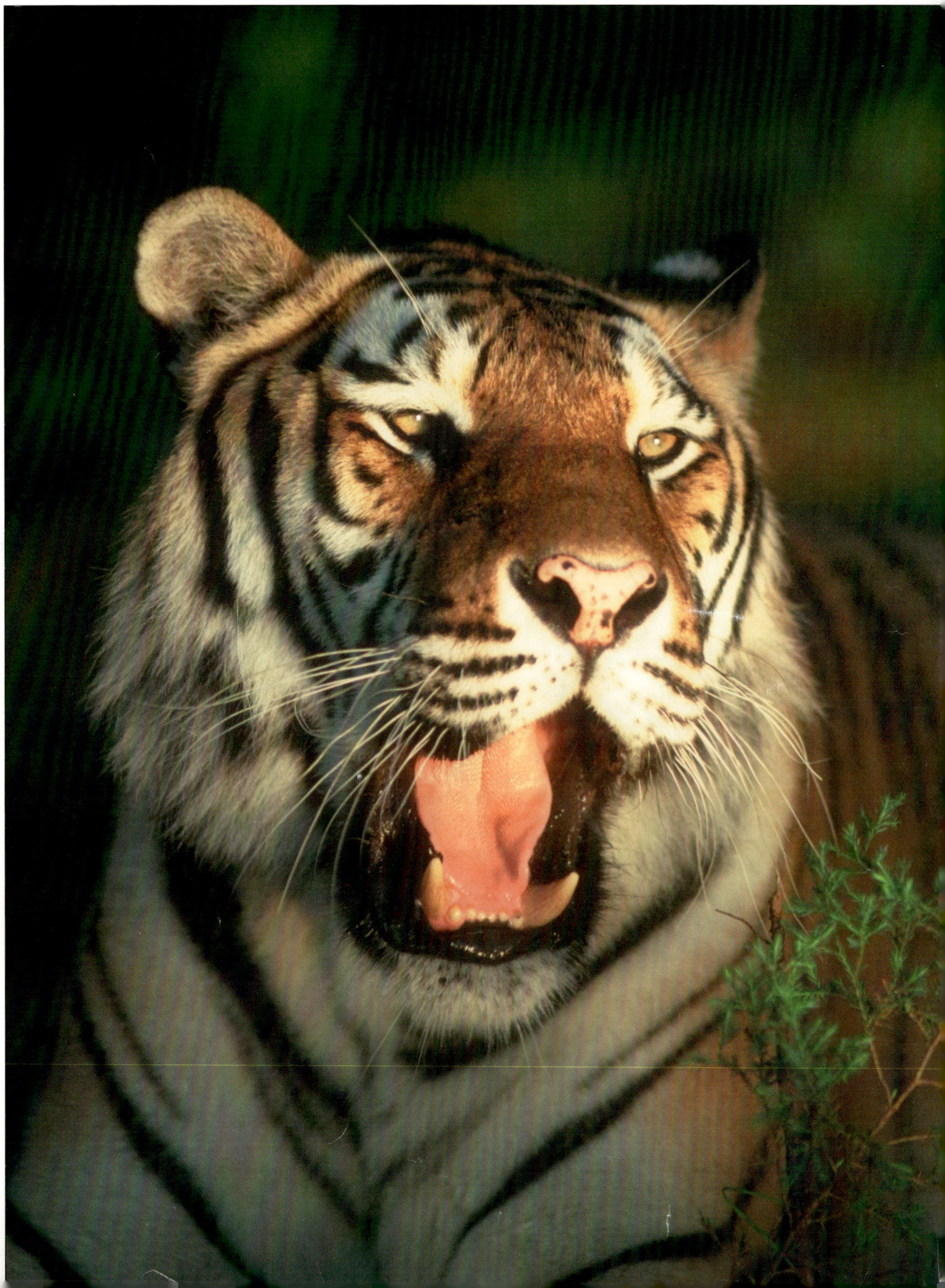

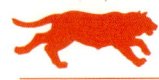

Features

One adult tiger can weigh more than four adult humans put together.

Opposite: The tiger is the largest of the 36 species of cats.

The tiger is one of the most recognizable animals in the world. Tigers are the only big cats to have striped coats. Their coats are mostly orange, with black or dark brown stripes.

Tigers are the largest species of cat. One adult tiger can weigh more than four adult humans put together. They have a large head with small, rounded ears. Their long tail is usually half the length of their head and body combined.

Tigers are powerful hunters. They are very muscular, with powerful shoulders and chests. Their teeth are 3.5 inches (8.9 cm) long. Tigers can eat as much as 40 pounds (18 kg) of meat at one time.

A tiger's tail is 3 to 4 feet (0.9 to 1.2 m) long, almost half as long as its body.

TIGERS

Ancestors

Today's big cats evolved from an animal called *pseudaelurus* that roamed Earth about 20 million years ago. The tiger itself evolved in eastern Asia. About one million years ago, groups of these animals began to move. They traveled into the southwest part of the continent in search of food and mates. These tigers developed into the Caspian subspecies. Some groups continued to travel and headed into India. Others took advantage of low water levels and crossed over to the Indonesian islands. These groups eventually evolved into the remaining subspecies.

The South China tiger looks most like these early ancestors. It also lives in the area where tigers are thought to have originated. Like the South China tiger, the eyes of these early tigers were set closely together and were quite forward. Their size was not remarkable. In fact, it is believed that the Siberian tiger of today is larger than any of its ancestors.

The Siberian tiger evolved from a smaller animal. Its larger size is a response to the cold environment in which it lives.

8

Classification

There are 36 species of wild cats in the world. Scientists have grouped these species according to size. There is a big cat group and a small cat group. The small cat group includes lynxes and cougars. The big cat group includes leopards, lions, jaguars, and tigers. Even though there is only one species of tiger, there are several subspecies.

Every known species and subspecies of animal is given a Latin name to describe it. This allows biologists from all over the world to understand exactly which animal is being discussed. The Latin name used for all tigers is *Panthera tigris*. Each word that follows *Panthera tigris* describes the subspecies of tiger.

SUBSPECIES

Biologists have divided tigers into eight subspecies. These subspecies are divided according to where each group of tigers lives. The following chart gives the common name of each subspecies and its Latin name.

Common Name	Latin Name	Where They Live
Bengal tiger	*Panthera tigris tigris*	Indian subcontinent
Caspian tiger	*Panthera tigris virgata*	Extinct
Siberian/Amur tiger	*Panthera tigris altaica*	Amur River region of Russia, China, and North Korea
Javan tiger	*Panthera tigris sondaica*	Extinct
South China tiger	*Panthera tigris amoyensis*	South-central China
Bali tiger	*Panthera tigris balica*	Extinct
Sumatran tiger	*Panthera tigris sumatrae*	Sumatra, Indonesia
Indo-Chinese tiger	*Panthera tigris corbetti*	Continental Southeast Asia

Size

Tigers range in size depending on the subspecies. The size of a particular tiger also depends on whether it is male or female, its age, and what it eats. Generally, adult male tigers are larger than adult females, called **tigresses**.

The largest tiger subspecies is the Siberian tiger. Adult males of this subspecies can weigh up to 675 pounds (306 kg) and grow to be 10.8 feet (3.3 m) long. Bengal tigers are also quite large. Adult males can weigh up to 569 pounds (258 kg) and measure 10 feet (3 m) long. The smallest living subspecies is the Sumatran tiger. Adult male Sumatran tigers weigh up to 309 pounds (140 kg) and can be up to 8.4 feet (2.6 m) in length. Extinct since 1950, the Bali tiger was the smallest subspecies. The largest Bali tigers were only 220 pounds (100 kg) and 7.5 feet (2.3 m) long.

The Siberian tiger is almost 11 times larger in length than a house cat.

LIFE SPAN

In the wild, tigers can live to be more than 15 years old. Although few live past 20 years in the wild, tigers in captivity can reach 26 years of age due to the availability of food and veterinary care. In the wild, older tigers may have worn or missing teeth and infections. Also, they may not be able to move as quickly as younger tigers. In captivity this is usually not a problem, but if its hunting skills fail in the wild, a tiger will not survive.

Fur

The striped coat of the tiger can be red-orange, yellow-orange, or brown-orange. Their belly fur is usually white. For most tigers, the fur on much of their chest and face is also white. The stripes are usually black, but can also be brown. No two tigers have the same striped pattern. The stripes on a tiger are even different on each side of its body and face.

Sometimes, white tigers are born. These tigers have brown stripes on top of off-white fur. Most of the white tigers in zoos are descended from one white male that was taken from the wild as a cub in India in 1951. Black tigers have also been reported, but only very rarely, and it seems that their coats are not all black. The one black coat that was taken from illegal traders in 1992 had black fur on the top of the head and back, but developed stripes farther down the body.

White tigers are found only in the Bengal subspecies.

Special Adaptations

Tigers have many **adaptations**, or features, that help them to survive the challenges of their environments.

Hearing

A tiger's hearing is very good. When it is hunting, the tiger uses this sense to locate sounds made by its prey. Like other cats, a tiger can move its ears to determine the direction from which a sound is coming. A tiger's hearing is important for communication with other tigers. A tigress must be able to hear her cubs calling in distress, and mates use their hearing to help find each other.

Sight

Tigers have **binocular vision.** Binocular vision means that both eyes face forward and focus on one object. It allows the tiger to better judge distance and makes the animal a better hunter. Humans, and most other meat-eating animals, have binocular vision as well. Tigers can also see very well in the dark. The shape of their large eyes takes in, or absorbs, plenty of light. This helps tigers see in the dark about six times better than humans, allowing them to stalk prey even at night.

A tiger is always on guard, using its keen hearing and sight to monitor its surroundings.

FEATURES

Smell

Tigers have a good sense of smell. This is important in tiger communication. Tigers sniff at scent markings to determine which tigers have traveled through their territories. They can use this information to avoid an area that is being used by another tiger and avoid confrontations. Tigers also use this scent information when searching for mates. Scent markings provide information on the sex and breeding condition of the tiger that left the mark.

Teeth

Tigers have 30 teeth. Their canine teeth are very big, compared to the size of their other teeth. The canine teeth are slightly curved and are usually between 3 and 3.5 inches (7.6 and 8.9 cm) long. Tigers use their large, powerful canine teeth for killing prey. A tiger chews its food, however, with its cheek teeth.

Tigers have a good sense of smell, but their sense of taste is believed to be non-existent.

More Special Adaptations

Legs

Tigers have hind legs that are longer and stronger than their front legs. This adaptation allows them to leap far distances. When hunting, tigers chase and then pounce onto fast-moving prey. Using its powerful hind legs, a tiger can jump up to 19.5 feet (5.9 m). The longest leap recorded for a tiger is 33 feet (10 m).

Paws

Tiger paws are completely covered with fur, except for the pads on the bottom. Both the pads and the fur allow the cats to stalk their prey silently. Tigers have long, sharp claws that are about 3 to 4 inches (7.6 to 10.2 cm) long. Like most other cats, tigers have **retractable claws**. All cats keep their claws pulled in while they walk, so that no claw marks are left with their pawprints. This feature helps keep their claws very sharp. Since they do not touch the ground while the tiger is walking, the claws will not wear down. Tigers use their claws to defend themselves and to hold onto their prey.

A tiger's claws stay sharp because they remain retracted when they are not being used.

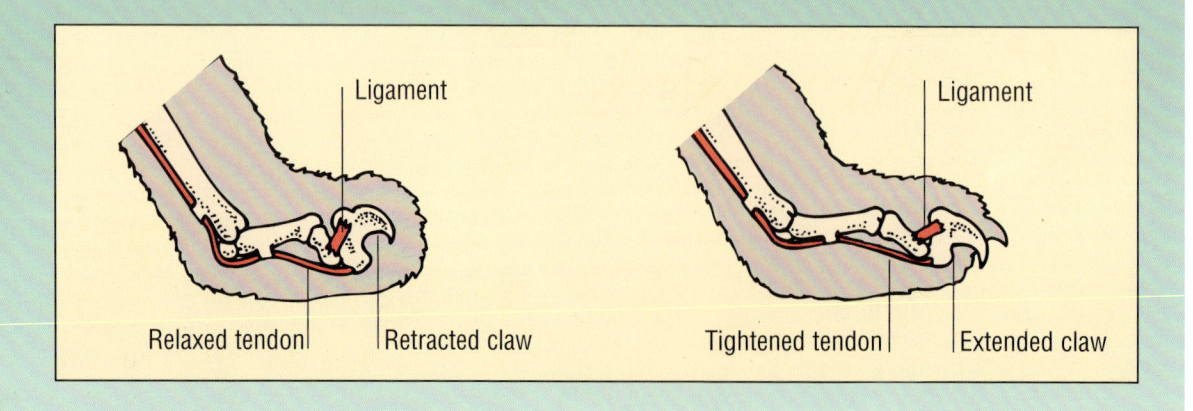

FEATURES

A Tiger Quiz

Try this quiz to find out how much you know about tigers. Are the following statements true or false? The answers are at the bottom of this page.

1 Tigers are the second largest cats in the world. Lions are the largest.

2 Tigers do not purr.

3 The Siberian tiger has the largest number of stripes of all the tiger subspecies.

4 The heaviest tiger ever recorded weighed 1,025 pounds (465 kg).

5 No two tigers have the same markings.

6 There is a subspecies of tiger that is all white.

Answers:
1) False. Tigers are the largest cats in the world.
2) True. Purring is a characteristic of small cats only.
3) False. The Sumatran tiger has the most stripes, while the Siberian tiger has the fewest stripes.
4) True. The tiger was a Siberian male.
5) True. The different stripe patterns may even differ on opposite sides of one tiger.
6) False. White tigers can be born in the same litter as normal-colored cubs.

15

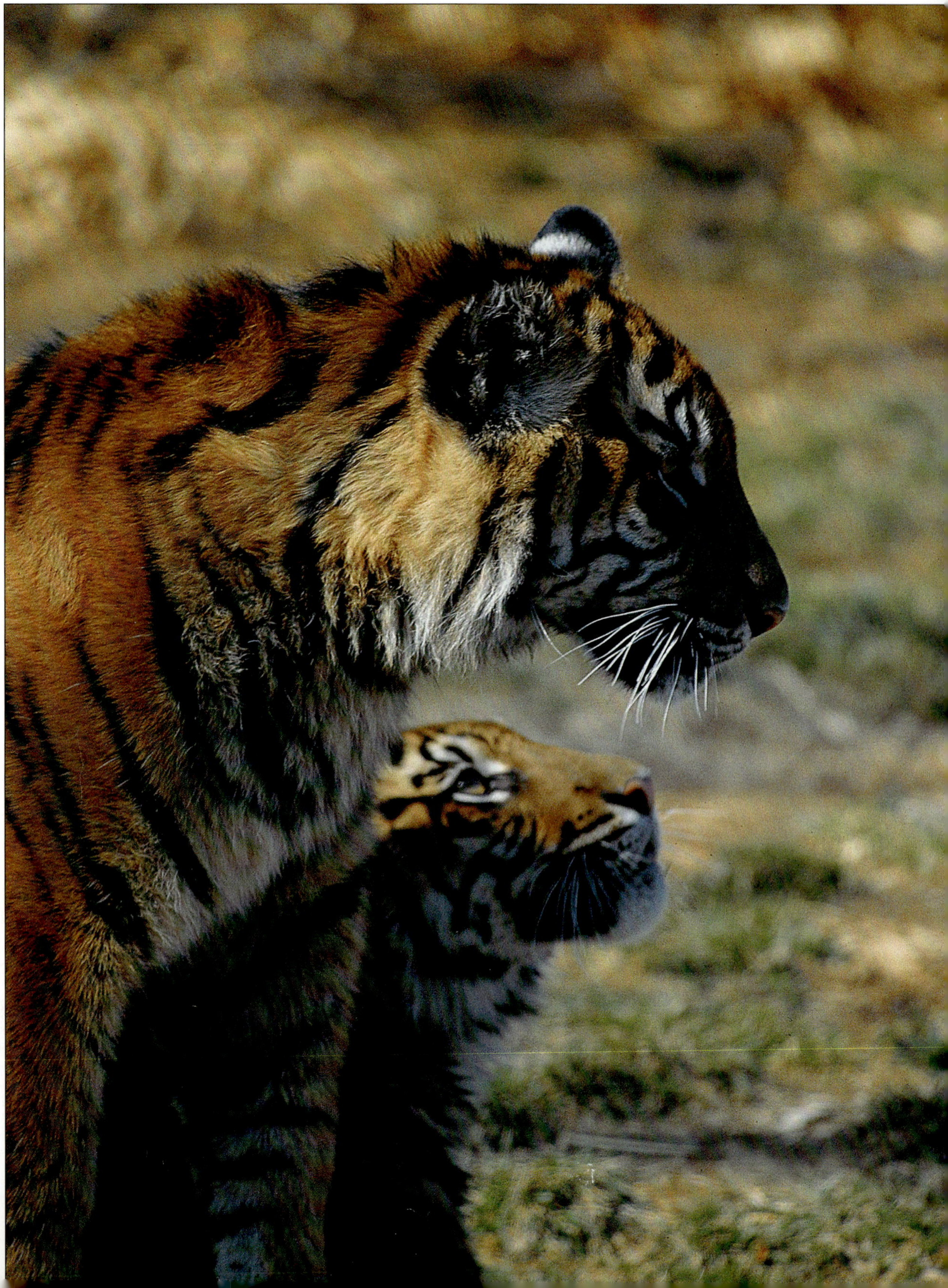

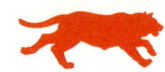

Social Activities

Although it is rare, tigers may hunt together.

Opposite: While normally solitary animals, tigers do come together for specific reasons.

Below: Even tigers have their playful moments.

Even though tigers usually live alone, they do interact socially with other tigers. Most of this interaction occurs indirectly, through scent and scratch markings. However, there are occasions when tigers interact directly with each other. During mating, a tiger and tigress will stay together for five to seven days. Male tigers are sometimes found with females and cubs when they are feeding or resting. Although it is rare, tigers may hunt together. In one instance, a group of two tigers and three tigresses were seen working together to hunt deer. Tigers will occasionally fight with other tigers.

Communication

Communication between tigers is very important. Cubs communicate with their mothers, competitors communicate with each other, and mates must find their partners before they can interact directly. Tigers use their senses of hearing, sight, and smell to communicate over long distances and when they are together.

Sounds

Tigers make a variety of sounds to communicate their wants and needs to other tigers. Snorting sounds, called prustens, are used when tigers meet each other in friendly situations. When tigers are being aggressive, they hiss and growl at each other. A moaning call is used to attract mates, while mewing sounds are mostly used by mothers and cubs.

A tiger often roars when it has killed a large animal or during the mating season. The classic roar of a tiger may be repeated three or four times in a row and may be heard from up to 1.8 miles (2.9 km) away. A moan is a quiet roar that can be heard up to 440 yards (400 m) away. A tiger also produces a coughing roar that is a short, loud sound made with its mouth open and its teeth bared. The coughing roar is made when the tiger is attacking.

Tigers hiss and growl to discourage others from getting close.

A tiger's roar can be very loud. Some roars have been recorded at 120 decibels. This is louder than a chain saw. A tiger's roar is also made up of **infrasounds**. These are low-frequency sounds that can be felt more than they can be heard. Infrasounds can cause a tiger's prey to become paralyzed momentarily.

SOCIAL ACTIVITIES

Scent Markings

Tigers, like other big cats, leave scent markings. These scent markings provide other tigers with information about the tiger that left the scent. The information includes whether the tiger is male or female, whether it is ready to mate, and the identity of the marking tiger. Most of these scents come from the tiger's urine, feces, and saliva. Other scents are made by glands on the tiger's chin, lips, and tail. A tiger will spray urine or will rub these glands on trees and other plants to mark its territory.

A tiger will also use its sharp, powerful claws to scratch the bark of trees or the ground. This leaves two claw marks and a scent marking from the sweat glands on its paws.

Tigers use scent markings to communicate with other tigers who may be trespassing on their territory.

More Communication

Body Language

Tigers also use body language to communicate with other tigers. A tiger that wants to show it is **submissive** will hiss and flatten its ears back tightly against its head. It may also flatten itself against the ground or back away, keeping low to the ground.

An aggressive tiger will do just the opposite. It will growl, hold its ears forward, stand up with its weight on its front legs, and swish its tail. It may even charge at another tiger and hit that tiger with its front paws.

Tigers may greet each other in a friendly manner by touching each other's cheeks or rubbing their necks or whole bodies against one another. This happens mostly when a mother greets her cubs or when adults are mating.

A tiger's body language can convey a range of moods and feelings, from anger to exhaustion.

SOCIAL ACTIVITIES

On a hot day, tigers relax by lying in a cool pond or stream.

Seasonal Activities

In the fall, tigers in northern climates grow a thick undercoat to prepare for the cold of winter. Winter coats are longer and fuller than summer coats. Winter fur can look very thick and sometimes even shaggy. It also appears more faded than summer fur. Tigers shed much of this heavy coat in the spring.

During the hot seasons, tigers cool off by lying in ponds and lakes. They seem to enjoy the water and are good swimmers.

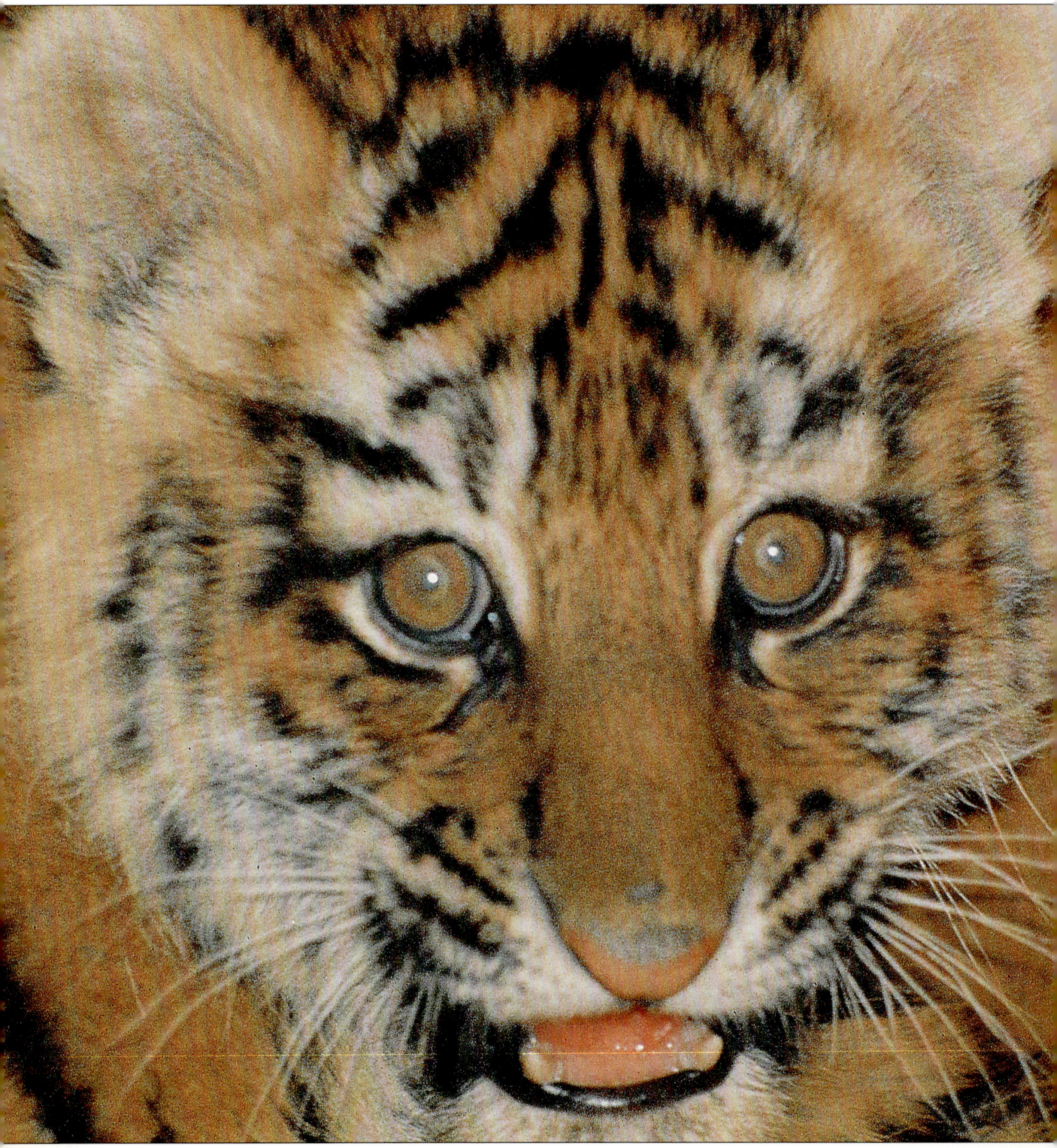

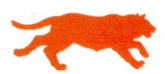

Tiger Cubs

Mother tigresses spend a great deal of time and energy preparing their young for the solitary life of an adult tiger.

Tigers may be powerful **predators** when they are adults, but at birth they are small and helpless. Mother tigresses spend a great deal of time and energy preparing their young for the solitary life of an adult tiger. They protect, feed, and teach their cubs to hunt and to survive on their own. The cubs stay with their mother until they are about 2 years old.

Opposite: Tiger cubs are vulnerable to many kinds of danger during their first few months of life.

Above: Mothers keep their cubs close until the cubs are able to take care of themselves.

Birth

Tigers can mate at any time of the year, but they usually mate between November and April. The **gestation period** for tigers is about 15 weeks. A tigress gives birth and raises her cubs by herself. A tigress usually gives birth to two or three cubs at a time. However, anywhere from one to four cubs can be born in a litter.

A tiger cub is born with its eyes and ears closed. A newborn cub has thick, woolly fur. It has a striped pattern like an adult tiger, but the fur is more lightly colored.

After mating, the male will return to his territory. He plays no further role in rearing the cubs.

TIGER CUBS

Care

To give birth, a tigress will find a sheltered area in tall grass, thick bush, a cave, or among rocks. She may make a covered nest out of leaves, grass, and fur.

During the first few days after birth, the mother will not leave her cubs at all. Then, she leaves them only briefly while she goes out to hunt.

For the first six to eight weeks of their lives, the cubs drink only their mother's milk. Later, they start to feed off the kills that their mother brings home.

Mothers and cubs stay close together until the cubs are 1 year old. When a cub reaches about 18 months of age, it may spend days away from its mother and is able to kill some prey. It may stay in its mother's territory until it is about 2.5 years old.

In her 15 to 20 years of life, a tigress can be expected to raise five to seven cubs.

25

TIGERS

Development

Birth to 12 Weeks

Newborn tigers are quite small, in contrast to their adult size. The combined head and body length of a newborn is only about 12 to 16 inches (30.5 to 40.2 cm), and it weighs only about 1.7 to 3.5 pounds (771 to 1587 g). Tiger cubs first open their eyes when they are between 6 and 14 days old, and their ears open when they are about 10 days old. Their milk teeth start to come in when they are about 2 or 3 weeks old. By the second month, the cubs have started to eat bits of solid food.

3 to 6 Months

During the first 6 months of life, a cub gains between one-quarter and three-quarters of a pound (0.1 to 0.3 kg) per day. A cub sheds its thick, lightly colored fur between 3.5 and 5 months of age. This fur is replaced by fur that has a background color darker than adult fur. By the fifth or sixth month, the cub starts to participate in hunts for food.

More female cubs live to adulthood than males.

TIGER CUBS

A tiger is born small but grows quickly, gaining almost 1 pound per day in its first 6 months. By the time it is 16 months of age, it will be able to tackle prey three times its own size.

6 Months to 1 Year

By 6 months of age, cubs stop nursing. Their permanent teeth start to come in at about 9 months of age. The mother teaches her young everything they need to know about hunting. This includes how to stalk, attack, and kill their prey.

1 to 3 Years

At 1 year of age, a cub weighs between 175 and 287 pounds (79 and 130 kg). By 18 months of age, the cub begins to make some of its own kills and is not as dependent on its mother. Between 2 and 3 years of age, the young tiger's fur takes on its adult coloration. At about 2 years of age, a cub will leave its mother.

28

Habitat

Tigers need an area that contains thick plant cover and enough large prey for them to eat.

Tigers live in the hot tropics of India (opposite) as well as the cold hinterland of Siberia (below).

Tigers are able to survive in many different types of habitats. In general, tigers need an area that contains thick plant cover and enough large prey for them to eat. Tigers' territories can include rain forests, wet evergreen and semi-evergreen forests, dry deciduous forests, bamboo thickets, tall grass jungles, shrublands, and even mangrove swamps. Tigers have also been found in areas with rocky mountain slopes and river valleys.

Tigers can survive extreme weather conditions in the winter, including deep snow and temperatures reaching below -40° Fahrenheit (-40° C). Tiger tracks have even been found in the snow of the Himalayan mountains, as high up as 9,800 feet (2,987 m).

Tiger Territories

A tiger's territory can be as small as 3.8 square miles (9.8 sq km) or as large as 193 square miles (500 sq km). The size of a tiger's territory depends on the condition of the habitat and on how much prey is available. Although tigers of the same sex generally avoid one another, they may share overlapping territories in a plentiful habitat.

A tigress lives and hunts within one large area. This is her territory, and she will try to keep other females out. When she has cubs, she raises them in her territory. In order to avoid dangerous fighting, females usually try to stay away from each other. They do this by marking the boundaries of their territory so that other females know they are there.

Male tigers also have territories. A male's territory is bigger than a female's, and often overlaps the territories of several females. In order to improve his mating opportunities, a male will try to make his territory bigger. He will fight neighboring males to do this. He will also have to defend his territory from young males looking for territories and mates.

In the cold mountain areas, a tiger's territory may be quite large because there are smaller numbers of prey.

On the Track of a Tiger

Although the tiger is the world's biggest cat, it is rarely seen in the wild. This is because there are so few of them, and those in the wild have learned to fear humans. To find these elusive animals, **poachers** and scientists look for the following evidence:

Tiger tracks are quite visible in snow-covered areas.

1. All tiger tracks have only four toe prints, even though tigers have five toes on their front paws and four on their back paws. The fifth toe on the front paw is raised above the others, so it does not touch the ground or make a print. Like most cat tracks, tiger tracks do not normally show any nail marks above the toes.

2. Scat, or feces, is often found along trails. It usually contains fur and bones from the tiger's prey. Since tigers eat many different species, the scat may also contain feathers, scales, or bits of turtle shell.

3. Scratch markings made by the tiger's powerful claws can often be seen on tree trunks and on the ground in tiger territory.

4. Dens, or lairs, may be found within a tiger's territory. These are places where the tiger regularly rests. Many tracks at the base of a hollow tree, at the entrance to a cave, or near a hollow under a fallen tree are signs that a lair is near.

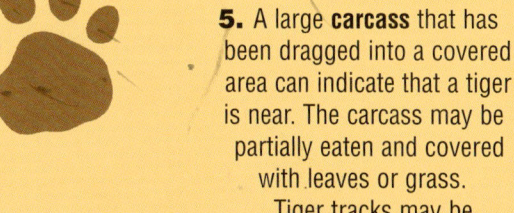

5. A large **carcass** that has been dragged into a covered area can indicate that a tiger is near. The carcass may be partially eaten and covered with leaves or grass. Tiger tracks may be found near the kill site and the carcass.

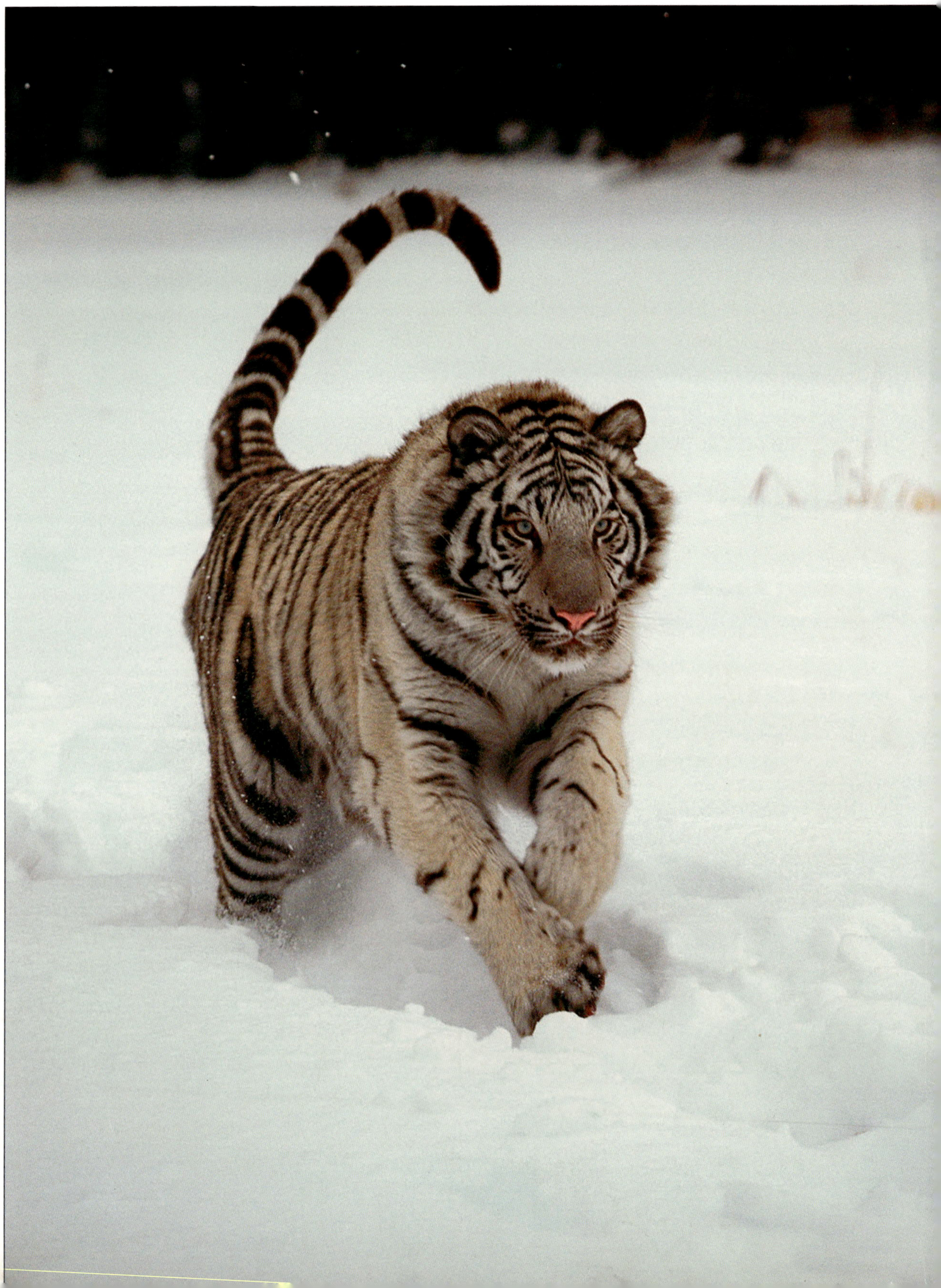

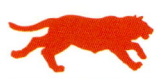

Food

Most of the tiger's hunts are unsuccessful.

Opposite: Charging tigers do not roar or make any other vocal sound.

Tigers spend most of their time searching for food. Most of their hunts are, however, unsuccessful. When a tiger does make a kill, it can eat a huge amount of meat at one time. After such a meal, the tiger will not need to eat again for days. Sometimes the prey is too big for even a tiger to eat in one sitting. When this occurs, the tiger feeds off the carcass for several days. When its favorite prey, such as deer, is available, a tiger will hunt mostly that animal. However, when food is scarce, it will eat whatever it finds—even frogs and porcupines.

A hungry tiger can consume as much as one-fifth of its body weight.

33

TIGERS

The gaur is very large prey for a tiger and is eaten over a period of 4 to 6 days.

What They Eat

A tiger's diet is made up mainly of large animals, but this depends on what prey is available in the tiger's territory. Tigers hunt mostly deer, buffaloes, and wild pigs. They also kill and eat gaur, an animal that can weigh up to 2,200 pounds (998 kg). Other prey includes tapirs, rats, porcupines, birds, and sometimes, other tigers. When necessary, a tiger will eat turtles, snakes, crocodiles, and fish. **Domestic animals**, including cows, goats, and dogs, can also become a tiger's prey. Tigers will feed on **carrion**, or dead animals, if they find them.

FOOD

Tiger Foods

Tigers are **carnivores**, which means that they eat other animals as their main source of food. Tigers usually eat larger mammals, but if they are hungry, they will also eat smaller animals. Tigers will sometimes also eat small amounts of vegetation, including grass.

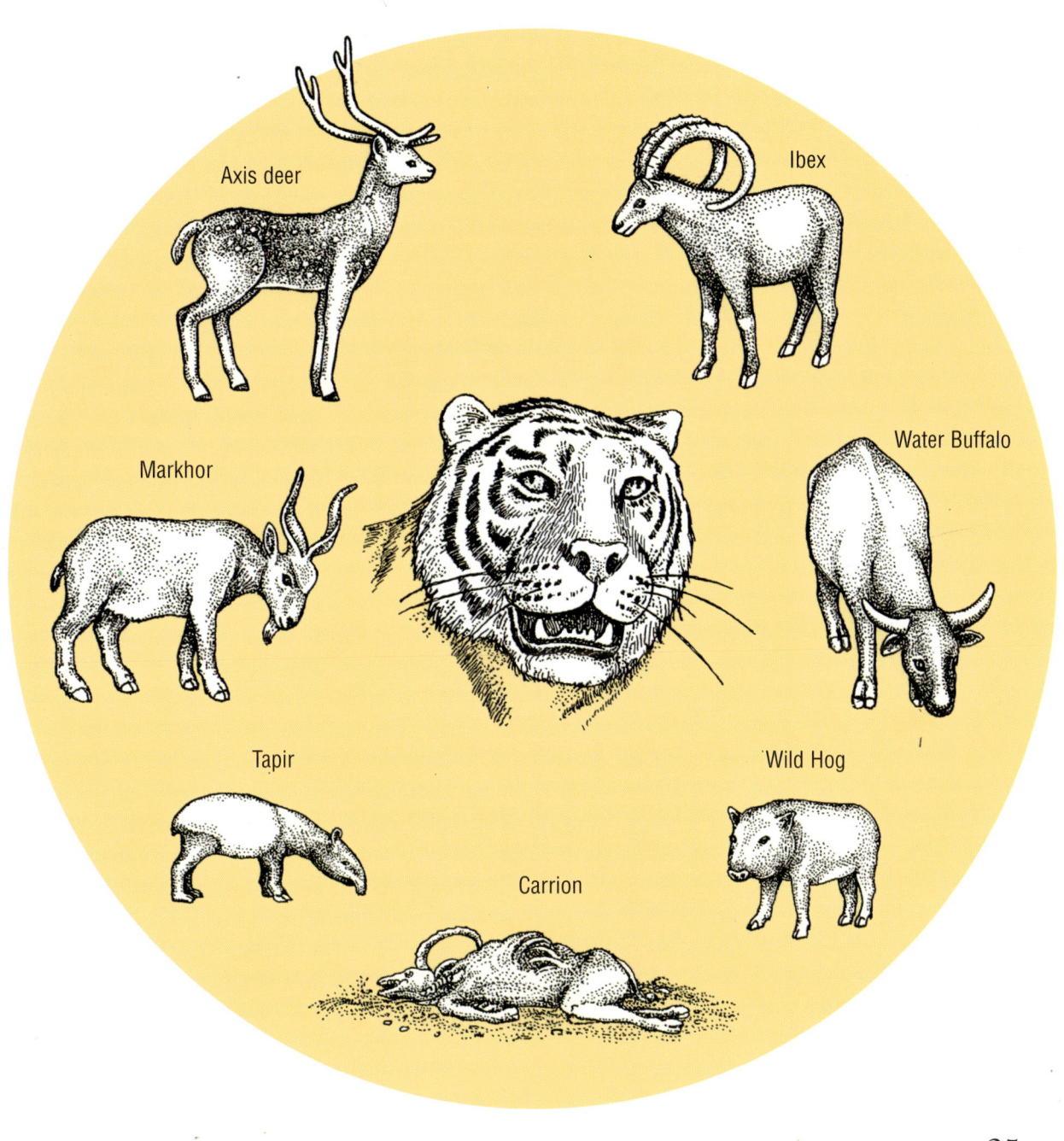

- Axis deer
- Ibex
- Markhor
- Water Buffalo
- Tapir
- Wild Hog
- Carrion

35

How They Hunt

Tigers hunt alone most of the time. They normally stalk their prey from behind or from the side, where the prey is less likely to see them. Tigers also try to stalk their prey from down-wind. This means that the wind is blowing in the direction from the prey toward the tiger, carrying the tiger's scent away from the prey. If a tiger is up-wind of its prey, the wind will carry the tiger's scent toward the prey, alerting it to the tiger's presence.

A tiger is a patient stalker and will not usually charge until its prey makes an abrupt movement.

When a tiger gets close enough to its prey, it will rush into it, knocking the other animal off its feet. A tiger almost always goes for the neck of the animal it is attacking. To kill large prey, a tiger bites the throat and holds on until the animal dies. This method of attack helps keep the tiger away from the horns or antlers of the larger prey. It also reduces the chance that the prey will stand up and defend itself against the tiger with its hoofs. To kill medium- and small-sized prey, tigers often bite right through the back of the animal's neck.

Once a kill has been made, the tiger will drag the carcass into a covered area to eat. If the carcass is not disturbed, the tiger may return to feed on it for three to six days after the kill. A tiger usually kills one large animal every week. Still, tigers often fail in their hunting attempts due to the speed and alertness of their prey. It is likely that only about one in twenty attempts are successful.

Tigers are **nocturnal** and do most of their hunting between dusk and dawn. In some areas, where they are protected from human hunters, tigers have been known to hunt during the day.

Wildlife Biologists Talk About Tigers

Maurice Hornocker

"Time is running out for the world's largest cat (the Siberian tiger). Reeling from the double punch of poachers and habitat loss, only a few hundred survive in the wild."

Maurice Hornocker's research has included both captive and wild Siberian tigers. He has been involved with the Siberian Tiger Project of the Hornocker Wildlife Institute since 1989.

Howard B. Quigley

"Clear-cutting and poaching are twin gun barrels pointed at the Siberian tiger. Once they roamed from Russia into China and Korea, but poaching and habitat loss have reduced Siberian tigers to fewer than 400 in the wild."

Howard B. Quigley has spent years studying big cats. He was part of a Russian–American team that cooperated on a three-year study of Siberian tigers.

U Tin Than

"In 2010 there will be Indo-Chinese tigers in Burma, but my country desperately needs more effective protected areas, management, and scientific studies of tiger population trends in those protected areas."

U Tin Than is a Burmese zoologist who works with the World Wide Fund for Nature in its Thailand Project Office.

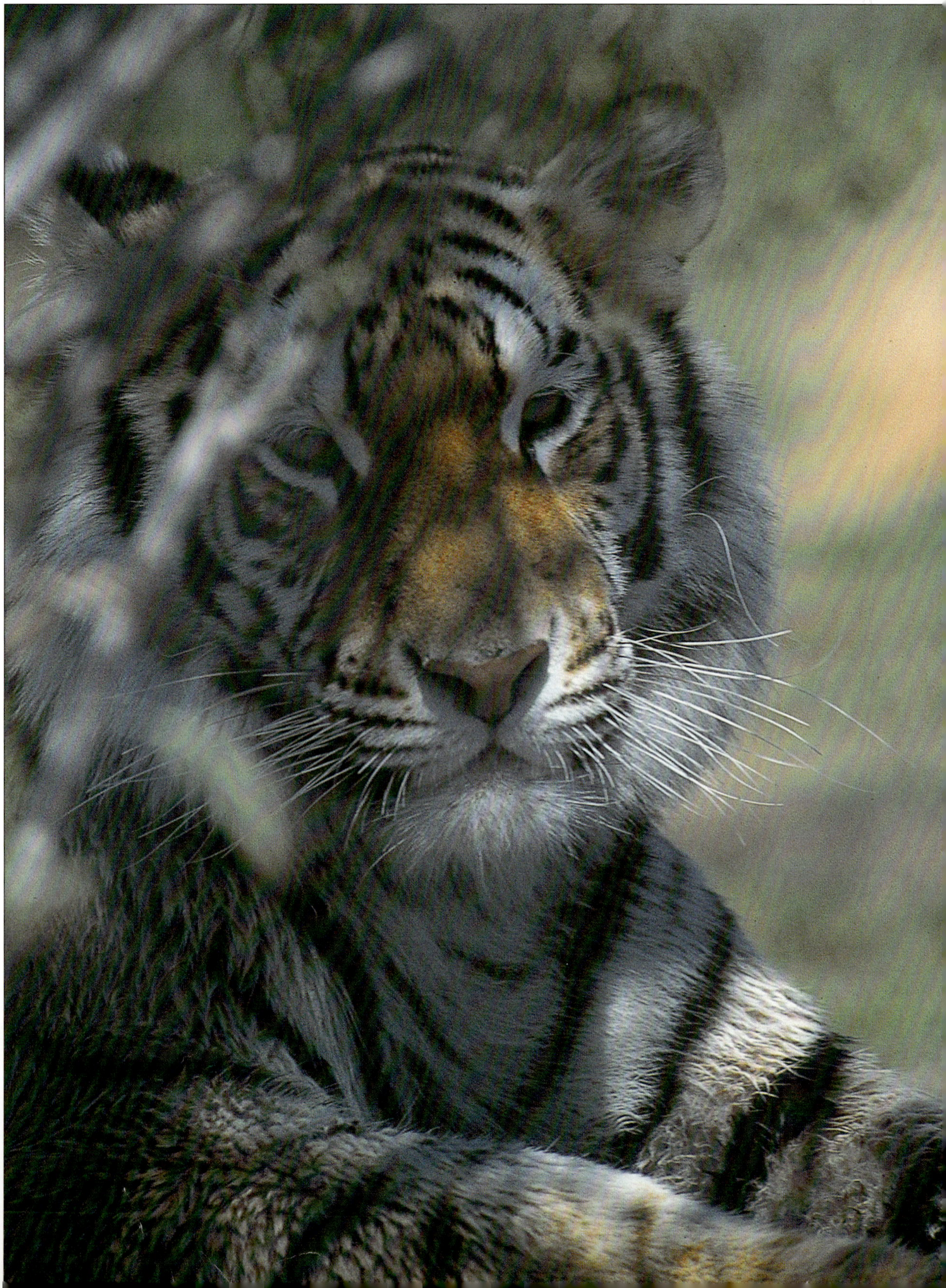

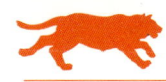

Competition

Large prey pose a special threat to tigers.

Opposite: Although tigers are fierce predators, they face an uncertain future.

Tigers must compete throughout their lives. They must compete for food and for territory. Both males and females will fight with other tigers over territories. Females will fight to defend their cubs. Adult males sometimes kill cubs.

Hunting is dangerous for the tigers, and they may get hurt in the hunt. Large prey pose a special threat to tigers. A tiger can get kicked with hoofs, stabbed with horns or tusks, or trampled during an attack. Despite all of the hazards within the animal kingdom, humans are the biggest threat to tigers.

Territorial confrontations can be violent and sometimes result in serious, or even fatal, injuries.

Competing with Humans

Humans are by far the biggest threat that tigers face. The tiger generates fear because it is known to kill both livestock and humans. To counter the threat, humans hunt, trap, and poison the big cat.

Killing a tiger has also been seen as a way of demonstrating human strength and power. In the early 1900s, wealthy European hunters and Indian **maharajahs** killed hundreds of tigers for sport. In fact, the Maharajah of Surguja was reported to have killed 1,100 tigers in his lifetime.

In the 1960s and 1970s, the commercial trade in tiger pelts was booming. During this period, one tiger pelt was bought for $4,250. In the 1970s, many countries began to realize that tigers were quickly disappearing. As a result, laws were put in place that helped slow the trade in pelts. Despite these efforts, the tiger is still being heavily poached to maintain the market for its other body parts, especially bone.

Tigers also compete with humans for their habitat. As human populations grow, forests are logged, tiger prey are hunted by humans, and tiger habitats are taken over by agriculture.

Tiger hunting was once considered a noble sport in India. The tigers would be gathered and herded toward the hunters, who were waiting on elephants.

Human-eating Tigers

At least 50 people are killed by tigers each year.

Tigers have killed more humans than any other cat species. In some cases humans have become the favorite prey of certain tigers. One tigress is believed to have killed 434 people in northern India before she was shot in the 1950s. Many tiger attacks have occurred in the Sundarbans mangrove forest, which fringes the Bay of Bengal in India and Bangladesh. In this region, tiger attacks on humans still occur each year. Most of these people are fishing, cutting wood, collecting honey, or harvesting prawns when the attack occurs.

Most tigers begin to prey on humans when it is difficult for them to catch their regular prey. A tiger may kill someone in defense and then continue to see humans as prey. Cubs may learn to hunt humans from their mothers.

Competing with Other Tigers

Although adult tigers sometimes fight, they are more likely to avoid each other. Occasionally, two tigresses will fight at the boundaries of their territories, or when one tigress is trying to move into another tigress's territory. A tigress will also fight another female when her cubs are threatened.

A male tiger will try to expand his territory so that he can mate with more females. He does this by fighting neighboring males. He will also defend his territory from young males that are looking for territories and mates.

Male tigers sometimes kill tiger cubs. These are likely the cubs of other males. In some areas, the main cause of tiger-cub death is due to adult male tigers.

Tigers are solitary animals that will not tolerate other tigers in their territory, especially when they are breeding.

Competing with Other Species

An adult tiger is far more predator than prey and does not compete with many other animals for food or habitat. Most tigers die of starvation or disease. Many others are killed by humans. In rare instances, bears, wild pigs, or large, hoofed animals will hurt a tiger so badly that it will die from its wounds. A tiger that hunts porcupines may get quills stuck around its mouth or in its paws. These wounds may become infected, and a tiger can occasionally die from them. There have even been cases when a tiger has been killed by an elephant or a herd of water buffaloes.

Tiger cubs are far more vulnerable to danger than adult tigers. Cubs can be killed by many other species, including jackals, hyenas, leopards, bears, and even eagles.

Hyenas normally feed off the remains of dead animals but will take advantage of a vulnerable cub if it is available.

Decline in Population

Tiger populations have dropped dramatically during the last 100 years. In the 1900s, there were up to 100,000 tigers in the world. Now there are only about 7,500 tigers left in the wild. Tiger populations have decreased as a result of three main reasons: habitat loss, the overhunting of tiger prey by humans, and commercial poaching of tigers.

Habitat Loss

Even if the hunting of tigers was completely halted, overall world tiger populations would still decrease. Many tiger habitats are continually lost as human populations grow and expand into what was once tiger territory. Forests that serve as home to tigers are now being logged. Agriculture is also spreading into regions where tigers live and hunt. In many areas, the loss of habitat has meant that tiger territories are becoming patchy. This means that tigers are becoming isolated from potential mating partners. As a result, these tiger populations may have inbreeding problems, such as weakened **immune systems**, and are likely to be affected more severely by poaching.

The habitat of the Siberian tiger is seriously threatened by logging.

COMPETITION

Signs labeling poachers the "enemy of the forest" are posted throughout Russia in an effort to discourage illegal hunting.

Overhunting of Tiger Prey

Humans have moved into much of the tiger's habitat. These people often hunt the same animals that the tiger hunts. This can cause tiger populations to decrease as not enough food remains to support both people and tigers. Tigers living in those areas may starve, or they may move into other areas and compete with resident tigers. Hungry tigers may also start to prey on humans or domestic animals. Such tigers are often killed for this behavior.

45

TIGERS

More Decline in Population

Trade of Tiger Parts

The illegal trading of tiger body parts is a major threat to this big cat. Poaching for these parts, especially tiger bone, is widespread, and is big business. Tiger bone is used mainly in traditional Asian medicines. Two thousand years ago in China, tiger flesh was believed to improve vitality and to help protect against demons. It has been used ever since. The tiger bone trade can be a profitable business. Just 2.2 pounds (1 kg) of tiger bone can sell for more than $1,000. One tiger can produce about 13 to 24 pounds (5.9 to 10.8 kg) of dried tiger bone.

Tiger bone is so popular that requests have been made to the Chinese and Thai governments to set up captive breeding centers so that tigers can be raised and killed for their parts. This practice is not approved by the Convention on International Trade of Endangered Species (CITES).

The single greatest threat to the survival of the tiger population is the tiger-bone market.

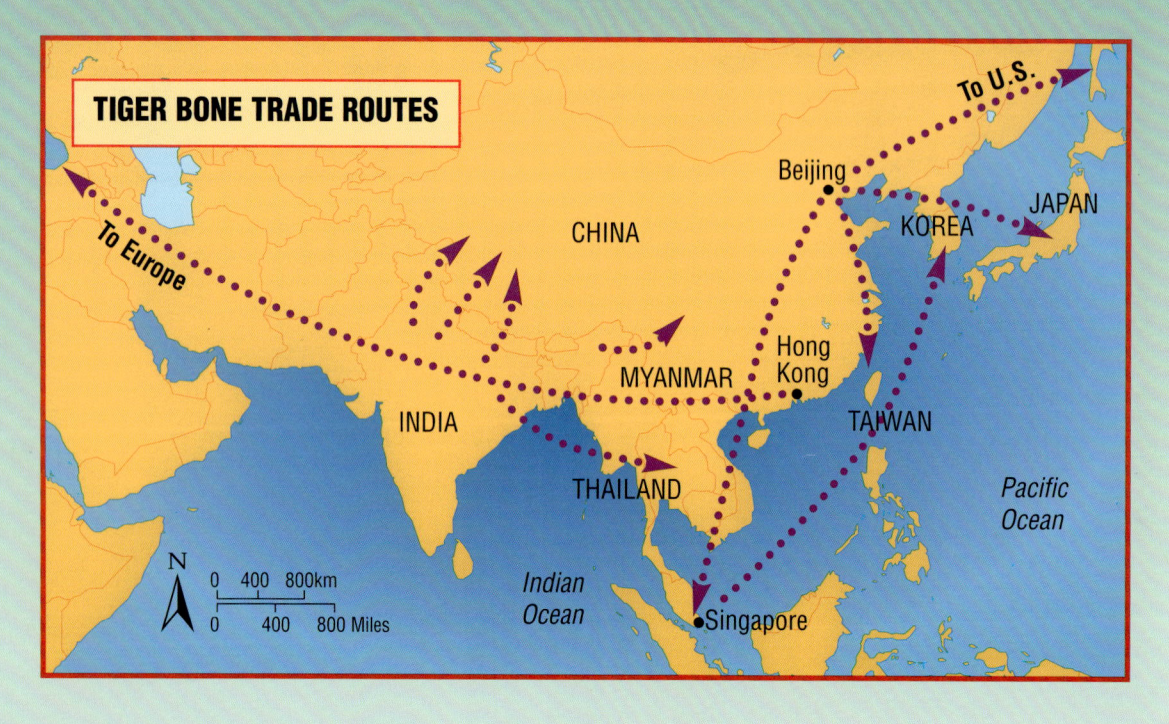

TIGER BONE TRADE ROUTES

Viewpoints

Should it be legal to sell tiger bone that is not from wild tigers?

There are currently more tigers in captivity than there are in the wild. Not only are tigers found in zoos, they are also bred at tiger farms, where farmers profit from selling the animals to zoos, circuses, and private owners. Some of these farmers have requested that they also be allowed to make money from the sale of tiger parts, meaning that they be allowed to kill tigers for the parts or to sell the parts when the tiger dies naturally. It has also been suggested that zoos could make money in much the same way, when tigers die at their facilities.

PRO

1 Tigers breed easily in captivity, and production could meet the demand for tiger bone. By producing a legal tiger bone supply, there will be less poaching on the wild tiger population.

2 If tiger farming were legalized, the price of tiger bone would go down. Poaching would no longer be as profitable as it is now.

3 Educational programs to stop the use of tiger bone will not work because the use of tiger bones in medicine is a tradition that has lasted for more than 2,000 years.

CON

1 Wild tigers may still be killed for their bones. Even if a tiger farm sells bone to be made into medicine, this will not stop a poacher from killing a wild tiger to make money for himself.

2 Many people do not agree with the commercial farming of an endangered species.

3 Instead of making tiger bone more available, campaigns should be targeted at the buyers of tiger-bone medicines. Human-made substitutes for the medical components in tiger bone should be pursued.

48

Folklore

Tigers have been worshiped and feared in many parts of the world. They play an important role in the folklore of countries such as India, China, and Malaysia. In these areas the tiger often represents strength and is considered "the king of beasts." Tigers are often portrayed as frightening and powerful animals in folktales. However, tigers are also sometimes seen as protectors. Ghost tigers are believed to guard graves in some cultures. Tiger images are used by some to guard against nightmares. Some people even use the body parts of dead tigers to guard against bad luck.

Opposite: In Indian folklore, Durga, the Goddess of Power, rides a tiger as a symbol of strength.

Tigers are not normally portrayed as being as friendly as Tigger, one of the characters in Winnie-the-Pooh.

49

Folktales

Tigers can be found in the folklore of the people who share habitats with the big cat. Tigers are both feared and honored. In some folktales, people and other animals often trick a tiger in order to save themselves.

Human-eating Tigers

"The Tiger, the Brahman, and the Jackal" is a tale told in India about a lying tiger who was tricked by a jackal. A man came upon a tiger caught in a trap. The tiger promised not to hurt the man if he would let him go. The man let him go, and the tiger announced that he was going to eat the man anyway. A jackal arrived and saved the man by tricking the tiger into getting back into the cage.

Haviland, Virginia. *Favorite Fairy Tales Told in India.* Toronto: Little, Brown and Company, 1973.

The Powerful Tiger

"The Competitive Tiger" is a story from China about a tiger who thought he was the most powerful animal in the region. He laughed at the other creatures. A bird showed the tiger that it could dance in the trees better than the tiger could. A small mole showed the tiger that it could get through a group of people better than the tiger could. Finally, a snail showed that it could get across a swamp better than the tiger could.

Jagendorf, M. A., and Virginia Weng. *The Magic Boat and Other Chinese Folk Stories.* New York: Vanguard Press, 1980.

FOLKLORE

A Rewarding Friendship

"The Hunter and the Tiger," a folktale from Siberia, describes a boy who is not afraid of anything. He traps a tiger and then lets it go because he feels sorry for it. The tiger becomes a boy and rewards his friend for his kindness.

Ginsburg, Mirra. *The Master of the Winds and Other Tales from Siberia.* New York: Crown Publishers, 1970.

A Big Transformation

"Tiger Woman" is based on a Chinese folk song about a woman who will not share her food with others. She says that this is because she is like a tiger when she is hungry. She is then transformed into a tiger and is chased away by men with spears. After being changed into a series of other animals, she realizes that she should share. She is then transformed back into a woman.

Yep, Laurence. *Tiger Woman.* Mexico: Bridge Water Books, 1995.

Braving the Tiger

The Chinese folktale "White Tiger, Blue Serpent" is about a boy who lives in a rocky, dreary land with dark and empty forests. A greedy goddess steals his mother's beautiful silk tapestry. He chases after it and braves a fierce white tiger and a huge sea serpent. In the end he finds the tapestry, and all the tapestry's animals, flowers, and trees come alive and make his land a beautiful place.

Tseng, Grace. *White Tiger, Blue Serpent.* New York: Lothrop, Lee & Shepard Books, 1999.

51

Folklore History

Many different cultures include the tiger in their myths and legends. Gods and goddesses sometimes transform themselves into tigers. Budhi Pallien is a forest goddess in North India, who travels the jungle in the form of a tiger. A tale from Bali tells of Leyak, who steals parts from human bodies to make a magic potion that changes him into a tiger. In China, Xi Wang-mu was originally a terrifying tiger-woman, who brought a plague to the people. She later became a beautiful goddess who represented immortality.

In many cases, the gods of myths ride on the back of a tiger. According to Chinese mythology, Zhu Rong, the god of fire, rides a tiger, and the Chinese god of prosperity, Cai-shen, rides a black tiger. In the Hindu culture, Devi is the mother goddess. She represents all women and rides a lion or a tiger when she fights against evil.

In other legends, creatures that are part tiger and part other animals are popular. Shachihoko is a Chinese sea monster with the head of a tiger. On land, it can change itself into a tiger. Baku, a good spirit from Japanese legend, has the body of a horse, the head of a lion, and the feet of a tiger. A person can ask Baku to eat a nightmare. By eating the nightmare, Baku turns it into good luck. These are just some of the many examples of tigers found in myths and legends.

The Shachihoko was used in medieval Japan as a gargoyle and can still be seen on top of some Japanese buildings.

Myths vs. Facts

Tigers are excellent hunters. Although tigers are powerful hunters, they are not always successful in their hunts. In fact, they are unsuccessful in most of their attacks. A tiger only kills prey once out of 20 tries.

Tigers do not like to get wet. Domestic cats have a reputation for avoiding water, but tigers enjoy it. During the hottest part of the day, tigers often cool down by lying in water. Tigers are excellent swimmers and have been known to cross rivers of over 18 miles (29 km) wide. A tiger might also attack a large animal, such as a crocodile or a deer, that is swimming in the water.

Tigers can be found in Africa. Contrary to common belief, tigers have never lived in Africa. Today's tigers are all descended from tigers that lived in south-central China. While tigers did move beyond China, there is no evidence that they ever ventured as far as Africa.

Past and Present Distribution

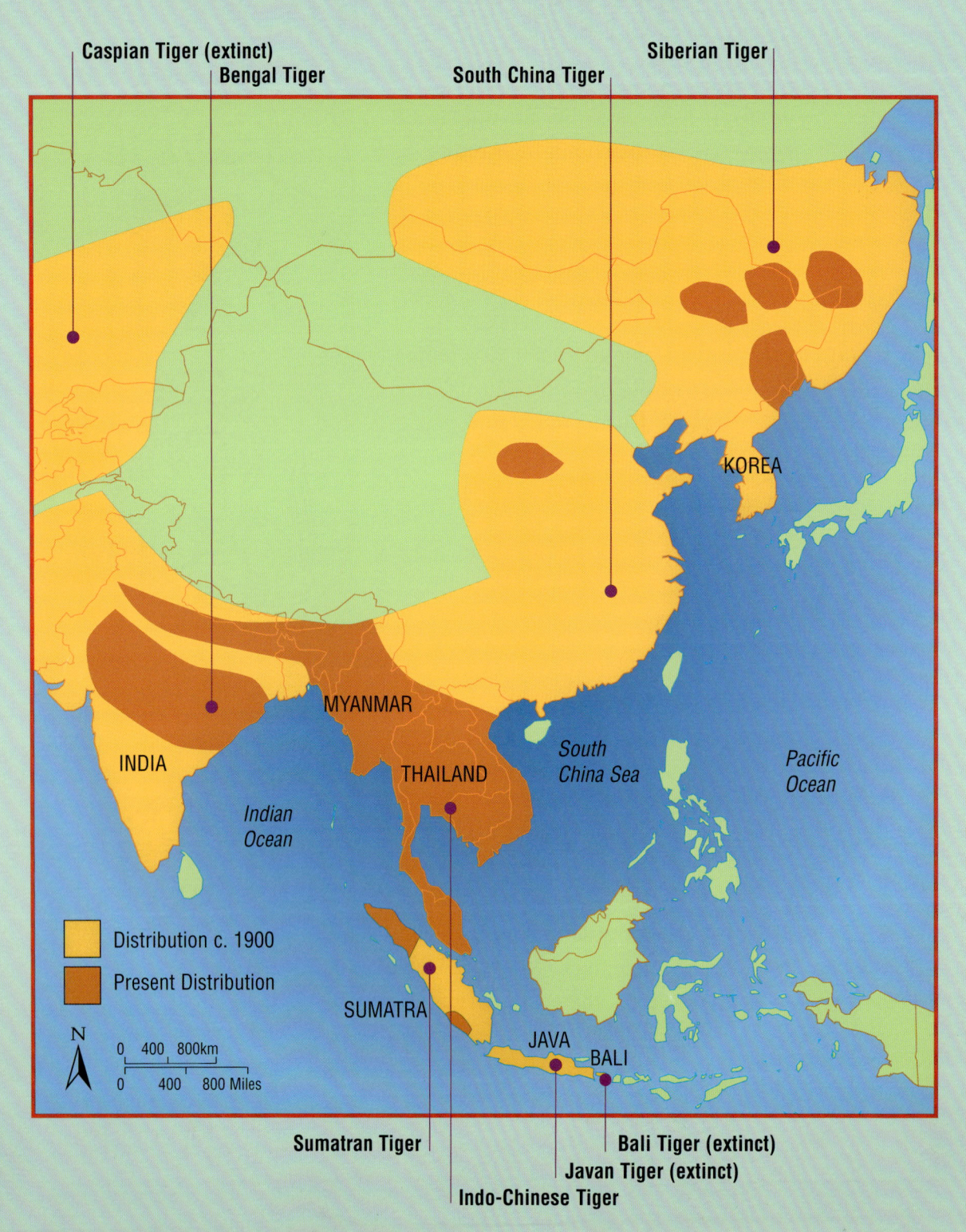

- Caspian Tiger (extinct)
- Bengal Tiger
- South China Tiger
- Siberian Tiger

KOREA
INDIA
MYANMAR
THAILAND
South China Sea
Indian Ocean
Pacific Ocean
SUMATRA
JAVA
BALI

Distribution c. 1900
Present Distribution

N 0   400   800km
   0   400   800 Miles

- Sumatran Tiger
- Indo-Chinese Tiger
- Javan Tiger (extinct)
- Bali Tiger (extinct)

Status

Tigers are found only in scattered populations from India to Vietnam, and in Sumatra, China, and the Russian Far East.

Opposite: Tigers live in isolated pockets of land. There are rarely more than a dozen tigers in any one area.

Tigers could once be found across Asia from eastern Turkey to Russia's Sea of Okhotsk. Today, tigers are found only in scattered populations from India to Vietnam, and in Sumatra, China, and the Russian Far East. Most of the world's tigers live in India.

The World Conservation Union (formerly named the IUCN) lists tigers as endangered. Of the eight subspecies, the Bengal and the Indo-Chinese tiger are considered endangered. The Siberian (Amur) tiger, the Sumatran tiger, and the South China tiger are considered critically endangered. Since 1975, tigers have been protected by the Convention on International Trade in Endangered Species of Fauna and Flora (CITES). CITES has banned international trade of tigers and their body parts for all subspecies of tigers since 1987. In spite of this, illegal trade continues worldwide.

Russian hunting societies have land reserved for the legal hunting of tigers.

TIGERS

Protecting Tigers

Scientists and conservationists track and study tigers to learn more about their survival needs.

There are many programs around the world that help save tigers. In 1972, the government of India started a large conservation program called Project Tiger. In 1900, there were about 40,000 tigers in India. By 1972, when Project Tiger was founded, there were fewer than 2,000 tigers. As part of Project Tiger, reserves were set up throughout India to protect the few tigers remaining and to help the population grow. These efforts were quite successful in the 1970s and 1980s. In 1979, there were more than 3,000 tigers reported in India. By 1989, there were more than 4,300. Unfortunately, in the 1990s, tiger poaching increased once again, and combined with the loss of habitat, the tiger population began to drop. Since 1989, India has lost between 200 and 300 tigers each year. It is now believed that there are only 2,000 to 3,000 tigers left in India. Project Tiger continues its efforts to protect India's tigers.

The Save The Tiger Fund is another program that helps tigers. Created in 1995, this fund targets projects that help conserve wild tigers in Asia. Since it began, the fund has supported 158 projects with more than $9.1 million. Public donations account for $1.4 million of this money. In 2001, the Save The Tiger Fund provided funding to 33 different projects.

To help protect tiger and rhinoceros populations worldwide, the United States Congress passed the Rhinoceros and Tiger Conservation Act of 1994. This act created a program through which tiger and rhinoceros conservation projects could receive funding. In 1999 and 2000, 51 grants were given to projects in 13 countries. The program gave more than $1 million to these projects.

There are many other conservation efforts that work with local communities and forestry departments. Some try to evaluate existing tiger and tiger-prey populations, while others work to protect tiger habitats, to reduce poaching and illegal trade, or to decrease human–tiger conflicts.

The Save The Tiger Fund provides funding to projects throughout Asia.

What You Can Do

You can help tigers by learning about them and teaching others about what you have learned. You can also help tigers by becoming involved with organizations that help protect these big cats and their natural habitats. Contact one of these organizations to learn more about how they are helping tigers.

Conservation Groups

INTERNATIONAL

IUCN–World Conservation Union
28 rue Mauvernes
CH-1196 Gland
Switzerland

World Wildlife Fund International
Avenue du Mont Blanc
CH-1196 Gland
Switzerland

Project Tiger
Government of India
Ministry of Environment & Forests
Annexe No. 5
Bikaner House
Shahjahan Road
New Delhi
110 011

UNITED STATES

Save The Tiger Fund
National Fish and Wildlife Foundation
1120 Connecticut Avenue NW
Suite 900
Washington, DC 20036

Hornocker Wildlife Institute
2023 Stadium Drive
Suite 1A
Bozeman, MT 59715

World Wildlife Fund United States
1250 24th Street NW
Washington, DC 20037

CANADA

International Society for Endangered Cats Canada Inc. (ISEC)
124 Lynnbrook Road SE
Calgary, AB
T2C 1S8

World Wildlife Fund Canada
90 Eglinton Avenue E.
Suite 504
Toronto, ON
M4P 2Z7

The Tiger Foundation
1066 West Hastings Street
Vancouver, BC
V6E 3X1

Twenty Fascinating Facts

1 A tiger's stripes are only on its fur and do not continue on its skin.

2 Without their fur, tigers and lions look exactly alike.

3 Tiger size is determined by where the cats are found. The largest tiger, the Siberian, is found much farther north than the smallest tiger, the Sumatran.

4 Like house cats, tigers spend much of their day sleeping. Between 16 and 20 hours each day is devoted to sleep.

5 Male tigers have an obvious ruff around their face. The ruff of a male Sumatran tiger is especially noticeable.

6 Tigers keep cool by lying in ponds or streams during the hottest part of the day. When they get up, they shake like a dog to remove the excess water in their fur.

7 A tiger's love of water is not natural. It is a learned behavior, taught to cubs at an early age by their mothers.

59

8 The saber-toothed tigers of prehistoric times were not actually tigers. Scientists agree that there was a type of cat that had saber-like teeth, but that it did not belong to the tiger family. These animals are now called "saber-toothed cats."

9 The Caspian, Bali, and Javan subspecies of tigers have been extinct since the 1970s.

10 When a 15-month-old Siberian tiger became stuck in a tree at a wild animal park in England, the park staff was not sure what to do. Climbing the tree to help the tiger could endanger the helpers. Darting the tiger with a drug could cause it to fall and injure itself. The staff decided to wait for the tiger to find its own way down. Five days passed before this happened.

11 A tiger's tail is about half the length of the animal's body. The tail helps the tiger keep its balance when negotiating a quick turn.

12 Even though a tiger's stripes are quite colorful, they may actually serve as camouflage, helping the cats to blend in with the shadows of tall grasses during the sunrise and sunset hunting hours.

13 The tiger's head stripes often form the Chinese mark of *wang*, meaning "king," on its forehead.

14 A female will not become a mother until she is 3 to 4 years old. Male tigers start to breed when they are 4 or 5 years old.

15 White tigers without stripes have existed. One such tiger was put on public display in London, England, in the early 19th century.

16 It is estimated that only about half of all tiger cubs born in the wild survive to be 2 years old. In many cases a whole litter is lost to fire or flooding.

17 Tigers do not form large groups the way lions do. Instead, they remain solitary and independent creatures.

18 White tigers are sometimes falsely called albino tigers. These tigers are not albino because they have striped markings and blue eyes. Albinos are white all over and have pink eyes.

19 Australia was once home to an animal called the Tasmanian tiger. With cat-like ears and stripes running along the back half of its body, it certainly resembled a tiger. The Tasmanian tiger, however, was a marsupial, meaning it was related more to a kangaroo than it was to a tiger.

20 In the Sundarbans mangrove, a program was started to help reduce the number of humans being attacked by tigers. Since tigers tend to attack from behind, people were given masks to wear on the back of their heads. In this way, a face is always watching a stalking tiger. The mask method worked to trick the tigers, and the attacks have decreased.

Glossary

adaptations: Changes made to fit into a certain environment

binocular vision: Both eyes can be focused on one thing. Binocular vision helps animals judge distance.

carcass: The dead body of an animal

carnivores: Animals that eat mainly the flesh and body parts of other animals

carrion: Dead and decaying flesh

domestic animals: Animals that have been tamed for the benefit of humans. Examples of domestic animals include dogs, cows, horses, and sheep.

endangered: A species in danger of extinction

gestation period: The length of time a female is pregnant

immune system: The system that protects the body from disease

infrasounds: Low-frequency sounds that humans cannot hear

maharajah: Title of some Indian princes

nocturnal: Active during the night

poachers: Hunters who hunt illegally

predators: Animals that live by killing other animals for food

retractable claws: Claws that can be pulled back into the paw when not in use. Most cats have retractable claws, but dogs have non-retractable claws that are permanently in an outstretched position.

scat: An animal's fecal droppings

submissive: Yielding to a power or authority; obedient

tigress: A female tiger

Suggested Reading

Guggisberg, C. A. W. *Wild Cats of the World*. New York: Taplinger Publishing, 1975.

Lumpkin, Susan. *Big Cats (Great Creatures of the World)*. New York: Facts on File, 1993.

Nowak, Ronald M. *Walker's Mammals of the World* (Sixth Edition). Baltimore, MD: John Hopkins University Press, 1999.

Nowell, Kristin, and Peter Jackson. *Status Survey and Conservation Action Plan: Wild Cats*. Switzerland: International Union for Conservation of Nature and Natural Resources, 1996.

Thapar, Valmik. *Tiger*. Austin, TX: Raintree Steck-Vaughn Publishers, 2000.

TIGERS ON THE INTERNET

One of the places you can find out more about tigers is on the Internet. Visit the following sites, or try searching on your own:

The Tiger Information Center
http://www.5tigers.org

Tiger Territory
http://www.lairweb.org.nz/tiger

The Tiger Foundation
http://www.tigerfdn.com

All for Tigers
http://www.tiger.to/aft

Index

ancestors 8

Bali tiger 9, 10, 54, 60
Bengal tiger 9, 10, 11, 54, 55
birth 23, 24, 25, 26
body language 20

Caspian tiger 8, 9, 54, 60
classification 9
coloration 7, 11, 15, 24, 26, 27
competition 39–47
conservation 55, 56, 57, 58
cubs 11, 12, 15, 17, 18, 20, 23–27, 30, 39, 41, 42, 43, 59, 61

development 26, 27

fighting 30, 42
folklore 49, 50, 52–53
folktales 49, 50–51
food 8, 13, 26, 33–37, 39, 43, 45
fur 11, 14, 21, 24, 26, 27, 59

gestation 24
habitat 29–31, 37, 39, 40, 43, 44, 45, 50, 55, 57, 58
hearing 12, 18
hunting 10, 12, 14, 17, 27, 36, 39, 44, 45, 60

inbreeding 44
Indo-Chinese tiger 9, 37, 54, 55

Javan tiger 9, 54, 60

legs 14, 20
life span 10

mating 17, 18, 20, 24

paws 14, 19, 20, 31, 43
poaching 37, 44, 46, 47, 56, 57
population 37, 44, 45, 46, 47, 55, 56, 57
Project Tiger 56, 58

scent markings 13, 17, 19
Siberian tiger 5, 8, 9, 10, 15, 37, 44, 45, 55, 59, 60
sight 12, 18
size 8, 9, 10, 26, 59
smell 13, 18
social activities 17–21
sounds 12, 18
South China tiger 8, 9, 54, 55
status 55–57
Sumatran tiger 9, 10, 15, 55, 59

teeth 7, 10, 13, 18, 26, 27
territory 19, 25, 29, 30, 31, 34, 39, 42, 44

water 21, 53, 59
weight 7, 10, 15, 20, 26, 27, 33